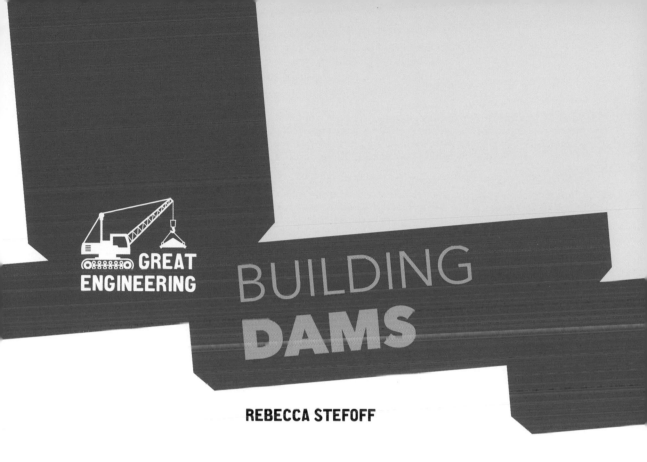

GREAT ENGINEERING

BUILDING
DAMS

REBECCA STEFOFF

Cavendish
Square

New York

Published in 2016 by Cavendish Square Publishing, LLC
243 5th Avenue, Suite 136, New York, NY 10016

Copyright © 2016 by Cavendish Square Publishing, LLC

First Edition

Website: cavendishsq.com

This publication represents the opinions and views of the author based on his or her personal experience, knowledge, and research. The information in this book serves as a general guide only. The author and publisher have used their best efforts in preparing this book and disclaim liability rising directly or indirectly from the use and application of this book.

CPSIA Compliance Information: Batch #WS15CSQ

All websites were available and accurate when this book was sent to press.

Library of Congress Cataloging-in-Publication Data

Stefoff, Rebecca, 1951- author.
Building dams / Rebecca Stefoff.
pages cm. — (Great engineering)
Includes bibliographical references and index.
ISBN 978-1-50260-595-5 (hardcover) ISBN 978-1-50260-594-8 (paperback) ISBN 978-1-50260-596-2 (ebook)
1. Dams—Juvenile literature. 2. Dams—Design and construction—Juvenile literature.
3. Civil engineering—Juvenile literature. I. Title.

TC540.S784 2016
627.8—dc23

2015004884

Editorial Director: David McNamara
Editor: Andrew Coddington
Copy Editor: Rebecca Rohan
Art Director: Jeffrey Talbot
Designer: Amy Greenan
Senior Production Manager: Jennifer Ryder-Talbot
Production Editor: Renni Johnson
Photo Research: J8 Media

The photographs in this book are used by permission and through the courtesy of: Andrew Zarivny/Shutterstock.com, cover; Zeljko Radojko/Shutterstock.com, 5; Robert McGuoey/All Canada Photos/Getty Images, 6; U.S. Army Corps of Engineers/File:Corps tests Hartwell Dam spillway gates (9372426574).jpg/Wikimedia Commons, 7; Drrfqq/File: Kallanai dam.jpg/Wikimedia Commons, 9; Gregory Heath, CSIRO File: CSIRO ScienceImage 4531 Aerial view of the Cataract Dam and Reservoir NSW 1999.jpg/Wikimedia Commons,11; Per-Olow Anderson/File: Abusimbel.jpg/Wikimedia Commons, 12; U.S. Navy photo Amy Hawkins/File:US Navy 060328-O-9999J-001 A wildlife biologist contracted by the Navy uses a dip net to sample tadpoles in a wetland at a Travis Air Force Base Firing Range.jpg/Wikimedia Commons,13; Bob Pool/Photographer's/Getty Images, 17; National Archives and Records Administration/File: Completed tunnel lining at intake portal of Diversion Tunnel No. 4,view looking toward entrance. Pressure grouting jumbo seen in operation NARA - 293757.tif18/Wikimedia Commons, 18; Snapgalleria/Shutterstock.com, 19; ChinaFotoPress/ChinaFotoPress via Getty Images, 21; Oceanfishing/Shutterstock.com, 23; Ernest Walter Histed (1889-1947) File: Debris at the P.R.R. stone bridge after the Johnstown Flood, by Ernest Walter Histed, May 31st, 1889.jpg/Wikimedia Commons, 25; Chris Wilson For The Washington Post via Getty Images, 27.

Printed in the United States of America

TABLE OF CONTENTS

CHAPTER ONE

Water Worries

People and beavers are alike in one way. But beavers are relatives of mice and rats. How are they like people? Beavers and people both build dams.

A **dam** is a barrier, or wall, that keeps water from flowing freely. When a dam blocks a stream or river, water builds up behind the dam. A pool or lake forms.

A river once flowed through this valley. Now a dam controls the river and makes a lake.

Some dams happen on their own. Frozen water can make an ice dam. Rocks and dirt can slide down a hill to block a creek.

Other dams were built by people or beavers. These dams are built to solve problems.

Beaver Builders

What are a beaver's problems? Why does a beaver need a dam?

Beavers are natural dam builders. Their dams can last for many years.

Beavers build dams to make ponds. The ponds are where beavers escape from bigger animals that might eat them, such as bears or coyotes. Beavers are good swimmers and can hide in their ponds, out of reach.

Ponds are also where beavers store their food. Beavers eat sticks and wood. In summer they drag food into their ponds and pile it on the bottom. Even if the top of the pond freezes in winter, the beaver will not have to leave the safe pond to find food.

To build a dam, a beaver cuts down trees with its sharp teeth. It drags the trees into a stream and stacks them. Then the beaver fills the holes between the logs with mud and stones. When the dam is solid, water makes a pond behind the dam.

Why People Build Dams

People build dams for three main reasons:

To store water. The lake that forms behind a dam is called a **reservoir**. People can use water from the reservoir for drinking and watering their crops.

To control water flow. Dams let people control a river and prevent floods. Dams have **spillways**,

Spillways are tested on a dam in Georgia.

channels that let water flow over the dam, or through it, or around it. Dam operators open and close the spillways. This feeds a controlled amount of water into the river below the dam.

To make electricity. As you will see in Chapter 3, many big modern dams make electric power.

Old and New Dams

The oldest human-made dams are in the Middle East and Africa. They are about five thousand years old.

Early dams were built of stones and earth that was piled up and then pounded until it became hard and solid. These dams were built to store water for use in the dry part of the year. A dam could help people live through the long, hard dry spells called **droughts**.

Some old dams are still in use today. One is the Kallanai Dam in India. It is more than 980 feet (300 meters) long and was built of stone almost two

The Kallanai Dam in India is almost two thousand years old. Concrete covers the old stones.

thousand years ago. A stone dam in Spain that was built by the ancient Romans is almost as old.

Today the largest dams are made of steel and **concrete**. Building a new dam is a big job.

CHAPTER TWO

Planning a Dam

Making a modern dam is no job for a beaver. It takes more than logs and mud. Even before the dam is built, there is a lot of work to do.

Before Building a Dam

The idea of a new dam brings many questions. Who will build it? How much will it cost? Will the dam hurt the environment?

Building a dam like this one in Australia takes a lot of time, teamwork, and money.

Big dams cost a lot to build. Most of them are built by governments. A government has enough money to build a dam. A government also says how land and rivers can be used.

Sometimes companies help pay for dams. If a company will get electric power from the dam, that company may help pay for the dam.

In the 1960s, Egyptian statues were moved to save them from being drowned by a new dam.

Scientists now know that dams change the environment in many ways.

Reservoirs swallow up forests and wetlands. Sometimes they drown whole towns or ancient ruins.

Wildlife can be harmed by dams. Salmon, a type of fish, swim up rivers to have their young. A dam might block their way.

Reservoirs hold a lot of **silt**—tiny bits of soil, sand, and rock particles. When a dam blocks a river, silt builds up in the bottom of the reservoir. When water from the reservoir is let out through spillways, the silt can kill fish eggs and hurt other wildlife.

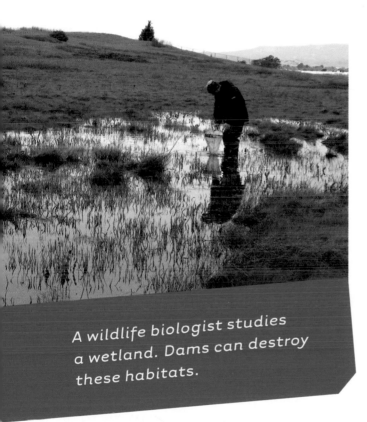

A wildlife biologist studies a wetland. Dams can destroy these habitats.

Today, no really big dams are being built in the United States. Worries about the environment are one reason. Another reason is that many rivers already have dams. But dams are still being built in other countries.

Engineers and Others

Once people have agreed to build a dam, they need a plan. The plan is made by a team with special skills and knowledge.

The most important members of the team are **engineers**. An engineer is someone who turns an idea into something people can use.

Engineers use science and math to solve problems. They create all kinds of things, from spacecraft to software programs for computers. An engineer who works on big projects for the public to use, such as dams and **tunnels**, is called a **civil engineer**.

Engineers know about the materials used in dams. They can tell how concrete and steel will act when the weather is burning hot or icy cold.

A **geologist** also helps plan the dam. Geologists are earth scientists. They study the place where the dam will be built. They ask, is there a chance of earthquakes or landslides? Will the ground hold up the dam?

A **hydrologist** helps, too. Hydrologists study the movement of water. They can tell how the dam will change the river, and how big the reservoir will be.

Making the Plan

The **engineering** team decides what shape the dam will be and what it will be made of. Some dams are straight walls of packed earth, with waterproof clay inside them. Others are tall, curved walls of concrete.

The engineers draw plans to see how the dam will look. They build small models of the dam and test them in running water.

Finally the engineers make a **blueprint** for the dam. This is a set of plans that shows every step in the making of the dam. The blueprint shows each piece of the dam, down to the last detail.

Now the dam is ready to be built.

CHAPTER **THREE**

Building a Dam

Dams are built in streams and rivers. How can workers build the dam with the river in their way?

Stopping the River

Dam builders have two main tools for getting the water out of the way.

One tool is the **cofferdam**. This is a huge metal box that is open on the top and bottom. The sides are watertight, which means that water cannot leak into the box.

The Bonneville Dam does two things. It controls the Columbia River, and it makes electricity.

The cofferdam is lowered into the river. It rests on the ground at the bottom. Pumps push water out of the cofferdam. Soon the inside of the cofferdam is dry. People can safely work inside it.

On the river bottom, the workers dig a hole. They fill it with steel bars and tons of concrete. Slowly they build the dam up from this solid base.

The other tool for getting water out of the way is called a **diversion channel**. This means making a

One of four diversion channels built around the Hoover Dam in the 1930s

new ditch or tunnel that goes around the dam.

The diversion channel carries the river away from where the work will happen. When the dam is done, the diversion channel is closed. The river goes back to its old path—but now there is a dam in its way.

In the 1930s, engineers built the Hoover Dam in a rocky valley in the American West. First they had to blast four diversion tunnels through solid rock. After the dam was built, parts of two tunnels were turned into spillways.

Energy from Water

Starting in the 1880s, engineers learned how to make electricity from flowing or falling water. Energy made this way is called **hydroelectricity**.

Water power for hydroelectricity can come from a natural waterfall, such as Niagara Falls. Or it can come from a big dam.

A hydroelectric dam has tall pipes built into it.

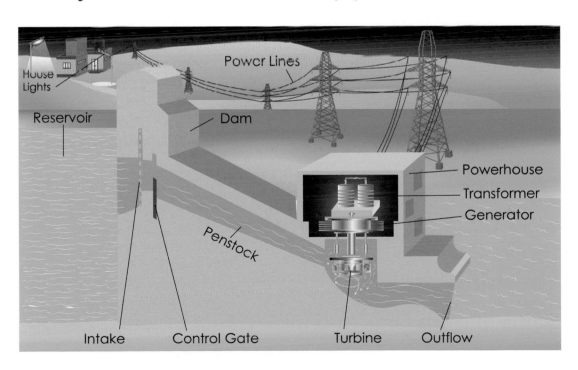

House Lights
Power Lines
Reservoir
Dam
Powerhouse
Transformer
Generator
Penstock
Intake
Control Gate
Turbine
Outflow

One end of the pipes is high up on the face of the dam that will hold the reservoir. The other end is low down on the other face of the dam.

Water flows into the pipes from the reservoir. It rushes down the pipes. At the bottom of the pipes, the water turns spinning blades, like big fan blades. They are fastened to poles. The blades turn the poles. At the top of each pole is a generator, a machine filled with magnets. As the magnets spin, they create electricity. Wires carry the electricity out of the generator.

Almost one-fifth of the energy used in the world today comes from waterpower. China, Canada, and Brazil make the most hydroelectricity.

Finishing the Dam

Dams that are large and thick take a lot of building material. The Three Gorges Dam in China is the

Floodwater pours through the spillways of the Three Gorges Dam in China.

world's biggest hydroelectric dam. It used enough steel to build sixty-three Eiffel Towers. It used more concrete than any other building project in history.

Once the dam is built, engineers and workers add the finishing touches. Sometimes they build a road so that people can drive across the top of the dam.

On a big river, engineers may add a ship lift—an elevator to carry ships from above the dam to below the dam. They may also build a railway to carry goods around the dam. Building a dam changes the land in many ways.

The River Is Tamed

Dams are amazing feats of engineering. Around the world they bring water and energy to people who need them. The reservoirs behind some dams are lakes where thousands of people swim and have fun. But dams also bring problems.

Whose Water Is It?

A dam changes the natural flow of a river. Places that used to get river water might get less water—or none.

Lake Mead is a reservoir on the Colorado River. When the water is very low, people can walk on part of the lake bottom.

In the American West, the Colorado River flows through five states and part of Mexico. Thirty-five million people or more use its water. The Colorado has fifteen main dams. The states that use its water have to divide it carefully. In times of drought, the river has less water for them to share. States have gone to court to sue each other for more water.

In Africa, the country of Ethiopia is building a huge dam on the Blue Nile River. That river flows from

Ethiopia into Egypt. Now Egypt is afraid that the dam will cause Egypt to lose up to one-quarter of its water.

People in India are also worried that dam-building in China will hurt them. That is because some rivers flow from China into India. Dams will let China keep more of the water for itself. As the world becomes warmer, fights over water and dams may break out.

Dam Disasters

Another problem with dams is the terrible flooding if a dam breaks. All of the water in the reservoir pours out at once.

A dam in Pennsylvania broke in 1889. The dam was made out of packed earth. Heavy rainfall swamped the reservoir and made the dam **collapse**. The flood killed more than 2,200 people.

Another 2,000 people died in Italy in 1963. This time the dam did not collapse. Instead, a big

A big flood in 1889 washed mud, trees, and houses against this Pennsylvania bridge.

landslide sent tons of rock into the reservoir. A giant wave splashed over the top of the dam into the valley below. Geologists had warned that there might be landslides. The dam builders did not listen.

Wild Waterways

Huge new dams are rising in some of the world's biggest rivers. In the United States, though, some dams are falling.

To help wildlife and the environment, some smaller dams are being taken apart. This is called dam removal. It lets the water flow freely again. Dam removal rebuilds the natural **habitat** of fish and other animals.

The biggest dam-removal project in history was in Washington State, on the Elwha River. Between 2011 and 2014 two dams were removed from the river.

Trees and bushes are now growing along the Elwha on what used to be the reservoir bottoms. For the first time in a hundred years, fish can swim up a natural, wild river from the ocean to give birth to their young.

Dams can help people in many ways. They can also do harm. Dam builders have to balance the good and the bad and make the best choice for everyone.

The Elwha River flows free, past part of a dam that was taken out. Fish can swim up the river again.

GLOSSARY

blueprint Detailed plan for building something, showing every step and every part.

civil engineer An engineer who makes bridges, dams, roads, and other structures for the public to use.

cofferdam A watertight metal box that keeps workers dry so that they can work on the bottom of the river.

collapse To fall down or break apart.

concrete A blend of sand, gravel, cement, and water that is hard and strong when it dries.

dam A barrier that keeps water from flowing freely.

diversion channel A passage made to carry river water around the place where the dam is being built.

drought A long dry period of no rain, or less rain than usual.

engineer Someone who uses science to plan and build things.

engineering The work of engineers.

geologist A scientist who studies geology, the subject of the earth and what it is made of.

habitat Place where a kind of animal can live.

hydrologist A scientist who studies water and the movement of water.

hydroelectricity Electric energy made from the force of falling water.

reservoir The pool or lake that forms behind a dam and stores water; a human-made lake.

silt Fine soil or dust that builds up in a reservoir when a dam blocks the flow of water.

spillway An opening or channel for water to flow over, around, or through a dam.

tunnel An enclosed passage that runs through the earth or under the water and has two open ends.

FIND OUT MORE

Books

Graham, Ian and David Antram. *You Wouldn't Want to Work On the Hoover Dam!* London: Franklin Watts, 2012.

Latham, Donna. *Canals and Dams: Investigate Feats of Engineering with 25 Projects.* White River Junction, VT: Nomad Press, 2013.

Weil, Ann. *The World's Most Amazing Dams.* Mankato, MN: Heinemann-Raintree, 2011.

Websites

Building Big: Dams

www.pbs.org/wgbh/buildingbig/dam/

Why Do People Build Dams?

www.damsafety.org/community/kids/?p=3e83ea84 -8035-4bac-b5ce-47fbd1ebc27c

INDEX

Page numbers in **boldface** are illustrations. Entries in **boldface** are glossary terms.

ABOUT THE AUTHOR

Rebecca Stefoff has written books for young readers on many topics in science, technology, and history. She is the author of the six-volume series Is It Science? (Cavendish Square, 2014) and the four-volume series Animal Behavior Revealed (Cavendish Square, 2014). She also wrote *The Telephone*, *The Camera*, *Submarines*, *The Microscope and Telescope*, and *Robots* for Cavendish Square's Great Inventions series. Stefoff lives in Portland, Oregon. You can learn more about Stefoff and her books for young people at www.rebeccastefoff.com.